BOOKS BY MARK STRAND

POEMS

The Late Hour *1978*
The Story of Our Lives *1973*
The Sargeantville Notebook *1973*
Darker *1970*
Reasons For Moving *1968*
Sleeping With One Eye Open *1964*

PROSE

The Monument *1978*

TRANSLATIONS

Souvenir of The Ancient World (POEMS BY CARLOS DRUMMOND DE ANDRADE) 1976
The Owl's Insomnia (POEMS BY RAFAEL ALBETRI) 1973
18 Poems from The Quechua 1971

ANTHOLOGIES

Another Republic (WITH CHARLES SIMIC) *1976*
New Poetry of Mexico (WITH OCTAVIO PAZ) *1970*
The Contemporary American Poets *1969*

THE LATE HOUR

THE LATE HOUR

MARK STRAND

ATHENEUM *New York* 1979

Poems in this book have appeared in the following magazines:

ANTAEUS: *Poor North; The Story*
FIELD: *Lines for Winter*
GEORGIA REVIEW: *Seven Days*
THE HAMPDEN-SYDNEY POETRY REVIEW: *No Particular Day; So You Say*
THE NEW YORK REVIEW OF BOOKS: *Exiles*
THE NEW YORKER: *The Coming of Light* (as *Late*); *Another Place; White; For Jessica, My Daughter; The Late Hour; About a Man; For Her; Where Are the Waters of Childhood; The House in French Village; Pot Roast; Night Pieces 1* (as *Night Piece*)
PLOUGHSHARES: *Snowfall* (in an earlier version as *Storm*)
SILO: *From the Long Sad Party*
TIMES LITERARY SUPPLEMENT: *My Son*
THE VANDERBILT POETRY REVIEW: *The Garden*
VIRGINIA QUARTERLY REVIEW: *Poems of Air; An Old Man Awake in His Own Death; Night Pieces 2* (as *Night Piece*)

The author wishes to thank the John Simon Guggenheim Memorial Foundation for a grant which enabled him to work on this book. He also thanks the Australia Council Literature Board and ANU for a fellowship during which time this book was completed.

Published simultaneously in Canada by McClelland and Stewart Ltd.
Library of Congress catalog card number 77-88904
ISBN 0-689-10977-6
Composition by Kingsport Press, Inc., Kingsport, Tennessee
Printed and bound by American Book-Stratford Press,
Saddle Brook, New Jersey
Designed by Kathleen Carey
First printing March 1978
Second printing January 1979

for

JULES

CONTENTS

Contents

III *Poor North*

IV *Night Pieces*

I

ANOTHER PLACE

THE COMING OF LIGHT

Even this late it happens:
the coming of love, the coming of light.
You wake and the candles are lit as if by themselves,
stars gather, dreams pour into your pillows,
sending up warm bouquets of air.
Even this late the bones of the body shine
and tomorrow's dust flares into breath.

ANOTHER PLACE

I walk
into what light
there is

not enough for blindness
or clear sight
of what is to come

yet I see
the water
the single boat
the man standing

he is not someone I know

this is another place
what light there is
spreads like a net
over nothing

what is to come
has come to this
before

this is the mirror
in which pain is asleep
this is the country
nobody visits

LINES FOR WINTER

for Ros Krauss

Tell yourself
as it gets cold and gray falls from the air
that you will go on
walking, hearing
the same tune no matter where
you find yourself—
inside the dome of dark
or under the cracking white
of the moon's gaze in a valley of snow.
Tonight as it gets cold
tell yourself
what you know which is nothing
but the tune your bones play
as you keep going. And you will be able
for once to lie down under the small fire
of winter stars.
And if it happens that you cannot
go on or turn back
and you find yourself
where you will be at the end,
tell yourself
in that final flowing of cold through your limbs
that you love what you are.

MY SON

(after Carlos Drummond de Andrade)

My son,
my only son,
the one I never had,
would be a man today.

He moves
in the wind,
fleshless, nameless.
Sometimes

he comes
and leans his head,
lighter than air
against my shoulder

and I ask him,
Son,
where do you stay,
where do you hide?

And he answers me
with a cold breath,
You never noticed
though I called

and called
and keep on calling
from a place
beyond,

beyond love,
where nothing,
everything,
wants to be born.

W H I T E

for Harold Bloom

Now in the middle of my life
all things are white.
I walk under the trees,
the frayed leaves,
the wide net of noon,
and the day is white.
And my breath is white,
drifting over the patches
of grass and fields of ice
into the high circles of light
As I walk, the darkness of
my steps is also white,
and my shadow blazes
under me. In all seasons
the silence where I find myself
and what I make of nothing are white,
the white of sorrow,
the white of death.
Even the night that calls
like a dark wish is white;
and in my sleep as I turn
in the weather of dreams
it is the white of my sheets
and white shades of the moon
drawn over my floor
that save me for morning.
And out of my waking
the circle of light widens,

it fills with trees, houses,
stretches of ice.
It reaches out. It rings
the eye with white.
All things are one.
All things are joined
even beyond the edge of sight.

FOR JESSICA, MY DAUGHTER

Tonight I walked,
lost in my own meditation,
and was afraid,
not of the labyrinth
that I have made of love and self
but of the dark and faraway.
I walked, hearing the wind in the trees,
feeling the cold against my skin,
but what I dwelled on
were the stars blazing
in the immense arc of sky.

Jessica, it is so much easier
to think of our lives,
as we move under the brief luster of leaves,
loving what we have,
than to think of how it is
such small beings as we
travel in the dark
with no visible way
or end in sight.

Yet there were times I remember
under the same sky
when the body's bones became light
and the wound of the skull
opened to receive
the cold rays of the cosmos,
and were, for an instant,

themselves the cosmos,
there were times when I could believe
we were the children of stars
and our words were made of the same
dust that flames in space,
times when I could feel in the lightness of breath
the weight of a whole day
come to rest.

But tonight
it is different.
Afraid of the dark
in which we drift or vanish altogether,
I imagine a light
that would not let us stray too far apart,
a secret moon or mirror,
a sheet of paper,
something you could carry
in the dark
when I am away.

II

FROM THE LONG SAD PARTY

FROM THE LONG SAD PARTY

Someone was saying
something about shadows covering the field, about
how things pass, how one sleeps towards morning
and the morning goes.

Someone was saying
how the wind dies down but comes back,
how shells are the coffins of wind
but the weather continues.

It was a long night
and someone said something about the moon shedding its
    white
on the cold field, that there was nothing ahead
but more of the same.

Someone mentioned
a city she had been in before the war, a room with two
    candles
against a wall, someone dancing, someone watching.
We began to believe

the night would not end.
Someone was saying the music was over and no one had
    noticed.
Then someone said something about the planets, about the
    stars,
how small they were, how far away.

THE LATE HOUR

A man walks towards town,
a slack breeze smelling of earth
and the raw green of trees blows at his back.

He drags the weight of his passion as if nothing were over,
as if the woman, now curled in bed beside her lover,
still cared for him.

She is awake and stares at scars of light
trapped in the panes of glass.
He stands under her window, calling her name;

he calls all night and it makes no difference.
It will happen again, he will come back wherever she is.
Again he will stand outside and imagine

her eyes opening in the dark
and see her rise to the window and peer down.
Again she will lie awake beside her lover

and hear the voice from somewhere in the dark.
Again the late hour, the moon and stars,
the wounds of night that heal without sound,

again the luminous wind of morning that comes before the
     sun.
And, finally, without warning or desire,
the lonely and the feckless end.

SEVEN DAYS

FIRST DAY

I sat in a room that was almost dark,
looking out to sea. There was a light on the water
that released a rainbow which landed near the stairs.
I was surprised to discover you at the end of it.

SECOND DAY

I sat in a beach chair surrounded by tall grass
so that only the top of my hat showed.
The sky kept shifting but the sunlight stayed.
It was a glass pillar filled with bright dust, and you were
    inside.

THIRD DAY

A comet with two tails appeared. You were between them
with your arms outspread as if you were keeping the tails
    apart.
I wished you would speak but you didn't. I knew then
that you might remain silent forever.

FOURTH DAY

This evening in my room there was a pool of pink light
that floated on the wooden floor and I thought of the night

you sailed away. I closed my eyes and tried to think
of ways we might be reconciled; I could not think of one.

FIFTH DAY

A light appeared and I thought the dawn had come.
But the light was in the mirror and became brighter
the closer I moved. You were staring at me.
I watched you until morning but you never spoke.

SIXTH DAY

It was in the afternoon but I was sure
there was moonlight trapped under the plates.
You were standing outside the window, saying, "Lift them
    up."
When I lifted them up the sea was dark,
the wind was from the west, and you were gone.

SEVENTH DAY

I went for a walk late at night wondering whether
you would come back. The air was warm and the odor of
    roses
made me think of the day you appeared in my room,
in a pool of light. Soon the moon would rise
and I hoped you would come. In the meantime I thought

of the old stars falling and the ashes of one thing and another.
I knew that I would be scattered among them,
that the dream of light would continue without me,
for it was never my dream, it was yours. And it was clear
in the dark of the seventh night that my time would come
soon.
I looked at the hill, I looked out over the calm water.
Already the moon was rising and you were here.

ABOUT A MAN

Would get up at night,
go to the mirror and ask:
Who's here?

Would turn, sink to his knees
and stare at snow falling blameless
in the night air.

Would cry:
Heaven, look down!
See? No one is here.

Would take off his clothes and say:
My flesh is a grave with nothing inside.

Would lean to the mirror:
You there, you, wake me,
tell me none of what I've said is true.

THE STORY

It is the old story: complaints about the moon
sinking into the sea, about stars in the first light fading,
about the lawn wet with dew, the lawn silver, the lawn cold.

It goes on and on: a man stares at his shadow
and says it's the ash of himself falling away, says his days
are the real black holes in space. But none of it's true.

You know the one I mean: it's the one about the minutes
    dying,
and the hours, and the years; it's the story I tell
about myself, about you, about everyone.

FOR HER

Let it be anywhere
on any night you wish,
in your room that is empty and dark

or down the street
or at those dim frontiers
you barely see, barely dream of.

You will not feel desire,
nothing will warn you,
no sudden wind, no stillness of air.

She will appear,
looking like someone you knew:
the friend who wasted her life,

the girl who sat under the palm tree.
Her bracelets will glitter,
becoming the lights

of a village you turned from years ago.

SO YOU SAY

It is all in the mind, you say, and has
nothing to do with happiness. The coming of cold,
the coming of heat, the mind has all the time in the world.
I wish the bottom of things were not so far away.

You take my arm and say something will happen,
something unusual for which we were always prepared,
like the sun arriving after a day in Asia,
like the moon departing after a night with us.

POEMS OF AIR

The poems of air are slowly dying;
too light for the page, too faint, too far away,
the ones we've called The Moon, The Stars, The Sun,
sink into the sea or slide behind the cooling trees
at the field's edge. The grave of light is everywhere.

Some summer day or winter night the poems will cease.
No one will weep, no one will look at the sky.
A heavy mist will fill the valleys,
an indelible dark will rain on the hills,
and nothing, not a single bird, will sing.

AN OLD MAN AWAKE IN HIS OWN DEATH

This is the place that was promised
when I went to sleep,
taken from me when I woke.

This is the place unknown to anyone,
where names of ships and stars
drift out of reach.

The mountains are not mountains anymore;
the sun is not the sun.
One tends to forget how it was;

I see myself, I see
the shine of darkness on my brow.
Once I was whole, once I was young . . .

As if it mattered now
and you could hear me
and the weather of this place would ever cease.

NO PARTICULAR DAY

Items of no
particular day
swarm down—

moves of the mind
that never quite
make it as poems:

like the way
you take me aside
and leave me

by the water
with its waves
knitted

like your sweater
like your brow;
moves of the mind

that take us
somewhere near
and leave us

combing the air
for signs
of change,

signs the sky

will break
and shower down

upon us
particular
ideas of light.

EXILES

Only they had escaped
to tell us how
the house had gone
and things had vanished,
how they lay in their beds
and were wakened by the wind
and saw the roof gone
and thought they were dreaming.
But the starry night
and the chill they felt were real.
And they looked around
and saw trees instead of walls.
When the sun rose
they saw nothing of their own.
Other houses were collapsing.
Other trees were falling.
They ran for the train
but the train had gone.
They ran to the river
but there were no boats.
They thought about us.
They would come here.
So they got to their feet
and started to run.
There were no birds.
The wind had died.
Their clothes were tattered

and fell to the ground.
So they ran
and covered themselves
with their hands
and shut their eyes
and imagined us
taking them in.
They could not hear
the sound of their footsteps.
They felt they were drifting.
All day they had run
and now could see nothing,
not even their hands.
Everything faded
around their voices
until only their voices were left,
telling the story.
And after the story,
their voices were gone.

2

They were not gone
and the story they told
was barely begun,
for when the air was silent
and everything faded
it meant only that these
exiles came
into a country

not their own,
into a radiance
without hope.
Having come too far,
they were frightened back
into the night of their origin.
And on their way back
they heard the footsteps
and felt the warmth
of the clothes they thought
had been lifted from them.
They ran by the boats at anchor,
hulking in the bay,
by the train waiting
under the melting frost of stars.
Their sighs were mixed
with the sighs of the wind.
And when the moon rose,
they were still going back.
And when the trees
and houses reappeared,
they saw what they wanted:
the return of their story
to where it began.
They saw it in the cold
room under the roof
chilled by moonlight.
They lay in their beds
and the shadows of the giant trees
brushed darkly against the walls.

III

POOR NORTH

POOR NORTH

It is cold, the snow is deep,
the wind beats around in its cage of trees,
clouds have the look of rags torn and soiled with use,
and starlings peck at the ice.
It is north, poor north. Nothing goes right.

The man of the house has gone to work,
selling chairs and sofas in a failing store.
His wife stays home and stares from the window into the
    trees,
trying to recall the life she lost, though it wasn't much.
White flowers of frost build up on the glass.

It is late in the day. Brants and Canada geese are asleep
on the waters of St. Margaret's Bay.
The man and his wife are out for a walk; see how they lean
into the wind; they turn up their collars
and the small puffs of their breath are carried away.

WHERE ARE THE WATERS OF CHILDHOOD?

See where the windows are boarded up,
where the gray siding shines in the sun and salt air
and the asphalt shingles on the roof have peeled or fallen off,
where tiers of oxeye daisies float on a sea of grass?
That's the place to begin.

Enter the kingdom of rot,
smell the damp plaster, step over the shattered glass,
the pockets of dust, the rags, the soiled remains of a mattress,
look at the rusted stove and sink, at the rectangular stain
on the wall where Winslow Homer's *Gulf Stream* hung.

Go to the room where your father and mother
would let themselves go in the drift and pitch of love,
and hear, if you can, the creak of their bed,
then go to the place where you hid.

Go to your room, to all the rooms whose cold, damp air you
    breathed,
to all the unwanted places where summer, fall, winter,
    spring,
seem the same unwanted season, where the trees you knew
    have died
and other trees have risen. Visit that other place
you barely recall, that other house half hidden.

See the two dogs burst into sight. When you leave,
they will cease, snuffed out in the glare of an earlier light.

34

Visit the neighbors down the block; he waters his lawn,
she sits on her porch, but not for long.
When you look again they are gone.

Keep going back, back to the field, flat and sealed in mist,
green the color of light sinking in ice. On the other side,
a man and a woman are waiting; they have come back,
your mother before she was gray, your father before he was
    white.

Now look at the North West Arm, how it glows a deep
    cerulean blue.
See the light on the grass, the one leaf burning, the cloud
that flares. You're almost there, in a moment your parents
will disappear, leaving you under the light of a vanished star,
under the dark of a star newly born. Now is the time.

Now you invent the boat of your flesh and set it upon the
    waters
and drift in the gradual swell, in the laboring salt.
Now you look down. The waters of childhood are there.

POT ROAST

I gaze upon the roast,
that is sliced and laid out
on my plate
and over it
I spoon the juices
of carrot and onion.
And for once I do not regret
the passage of time.

I sit by a window
that looks
on the soot-stained brick of buildings
and do not care that I see
no living thing—not a bird,
not a branch in bloom,
not a soul moving
in the rooms
behind the dark panes.
These days when there is little
to love or to praise
one could do worse
than yield
to the power of food.
So I bend

to inhale
the steam that rises
from my plate, and I think
of the first time

I tasted a roast
like this.
It was years ago
in Seabright,
Nova Scotia;
my mother leaned
over my dish and filled it
and when I finished
filled it again.
I remember the gravy,
its odor of garlic and celery,
and sopping it up
with pieces of bread.

And now
I taste it again.
The meat of memory.
The meat of no change.
I raise my fork in praise,
and I eat.

THE HOUSE IN FRENCH VILLAGE

for Elizabeth Bishop

It stood by itself
in a sloping field,
it was white
with green
shutters and trim,

and its gambrel roof
gave it the look
of a small
prim barn.
From the porch

when the weather was clear,
I could see Fox Point,
across the bay
where the fishermen,
I was told,

laid out
their catch of tuna
on the pier
and hacked away with axes
at the bellies

of the giant fish.
I would stare
at Wedge Island

where gulls wheeled
in loud broken rings

above their young;
at Albert Hubley's shack
built over water, and sagging;
at Boutelier's wharf
loaded down

with barrels of brine
and nets to be mended.
I would sit
with my grandmother,
my aunt, and my mother,

the four of us rocking
on chairs, watching
the narrow dirt road
for a sign
of the black

baby Austin
my father would drive
to town and back.
But the weather
was not often clear

and all we could see
were sheets of cold rain
sweeping this way and that,

riffling the sea's coat
of deep green,

and the wind
beating the field flat,
sending up to the porch
gusts of salt spray
that carried

the odor of fish
and the rot,
so it seemed,
of the whole bay,
while we kept watch.

THE GARDEN

for Robert Penn Warren

It shines in the garden,
in the white foliage of the chestnut tree,
in the brim of my father's hat
as he walks on the gravel.

In the garden suspended in time
my mother sits in a redwood chair;
light fills the sky,
the folds of her dress,
the roses tangled beside her.

And when my father bends
to whisper in her ear,
when they rise to leave
and the swallows dip and soar
and the moon and stars
have drifted off together, it shines.

Even as you lean over this page,
late and alone, it shines; even now
in the moment before it disappears.

SNOWFALL

Watching snow cover the ground, cover itself,
cover everything that is not you, you see
it is the downward drift of light
upon the sound of air sweeping away the air,
it is the fall of moments into moments, the burial
of sleep, the down of winter, the negative of night.

IV

NIGHT PIECES

NIGHT PIECES

for Bill and Sandy Bailey

I
(after Dickens)

A fine bright moon and thousands of stars!
It is a still night, a very still night
and the stillness is everywhere.

Not only is it a still night
on deserted roads and hilltops
where the dim, quilted countryside seems to doze
as it fans out into clumps of trees dark and unbending
against the sky, with the gray dust of moonlight upon them,

not only is it a still night
in backyards overgrown with weeds, and in woods,
and by tracks where the rat sleeps under the garnet-crusted
    rock,
and in the abandoned station that reeks of mildew and urine,
and on the river where the oil slick rides the current
sparkling among islands and scattered weirs,

not only is it a still night
where the river winds through marshes and mudflats fouled
by bottles, tires and rusty cans, and where it narrows
through the sloping acres of higher ground covered with
    plots
cleared and graded for building,

not only is it a still night
wherever the river flows, where houses cluster in small towns,
but farther down where more and more bridges are reflected
    in it,
where wharves, cranes, warehouses, make it black and awful,
where it turns from those creaking shapes and mingles with
    the sea,

and not only is it a still night
at sea and on the pale glass of the beach
where the watcher stands upright in the mystery and motion
    of his life
and sees the silent ships move in from nowhere he has ever
    been,
crossing the path of light that he believes runs only to him,

but even in this stranger's wilderness of a city
it is a still night. Steeples and skyscrapers grow
more ethereal, rooftops crowded with towers and ducts
lose their ugliness under the shining of the urban moon;
street noises are fewer and are softened, and footsteps
on the sidewalks pass more quietly away.

In this place where the sound of sirens never ceases
and people move like a ghostly traffic from home to work
    and home,
and the poor in their tenements speak to their gods
and the rich do not hear them, every sound is merged,
this moonlit night, into a distant humming, as if
the city, finally, were singing itself to sleep.

I I
(*after Carlos Drummond de Andrade*)

It is night. I feel it is night
not because darkness has fallen
(what do I care about darkness falling)
but because down in myself the shouting
has stopped, has given up.
I feel we are night,
that we sink into dark
and dissolve into night.
I feel it is night in the wind,
night in the sea, in the stone,
in the harp of the angel who sings to me.
And turning on lights wouldn't help,
and taking my hand wouldn't help. Not now.
It is night where Jess lies down,
where Phil and Fran are asleep,
night for the Simics, night for the Baileys,
night for Dan, for Richard, for Sandy.
For all my friends it is night,
and in all my friends it is night.
It is night, not death, it is night
filling up sleep without dreams,
without stars. It is night,
not pain or rest, it is night,

the perfection of night.
It is night that changes

now in the first glimpse of day,
in the ribbons of rising light,
and the world assembles itself once more.
In the park someone is running,
someone is walking his dog.
For whatever reason, people are waking.
Someone is cooking, someone
is bringing The Times to the door.
Streets are filling with light.
My friends are rubbing the sleep from their eyes.
Jules is rubbing the sleep from her eyes,
and I sit at the table
drinking my morning coffee.
All that we lost at night is back.
Thank you, faithful things!
Thank you, world!
To know that the city is still there,
that the woods are still there,
and the houses, and the humming of traffic,
and the slow cows grazing in the field;
that the earth continues to turn
and time hasn't stopped,
that we come back whole
to suck the sweet marrow of day,
thank you, bright morning,
thank you, thank you!

Mark Strand was born in Summerside, Prince Edward Island, Canada, but has lived most of his life in the United States. He has taught at numerous colleges and universities, including Columbia, Princeton, University of Virginia, University of Washington and Brandeis. He has been a Fulbright Scholar to Italy and has received grants from The National Endowment for the Arts, the Rockefeller Foundation, and the Guggenheim Foundation. In 1974 he became the first recipient of the Edgar Allan Poe Award and in 1975 he received an award from The National Institute of Arts and Letters and The American Academy of Arts and Letters. THE LATE HOUR is Mark Strand's sixth book of poems.